"Steve Eggleton invites the rea[...]
his effective use of scripture m[...]
of John's life in God's Big Stor[...]

**Bob Hartman, author and performance storyteller**

# GOD
## and
# NOAH
## Save the
# WORLD

## Steve Eggleton

LION
CHILDREN'S

Published by **Lion Children's**
www.lionhudson.com
Part of the SPCK Group
SPCK, 36 Causton Street, London SW1P 4ST

ISBN 978 0 74597 877 2
e-ISBN 978 0 74597 878 9

First edition 2022

A catalogue record for this book is available from the British Library

Printed and bound in the UK, September 2021, LH26

# Contents

# Family Tree

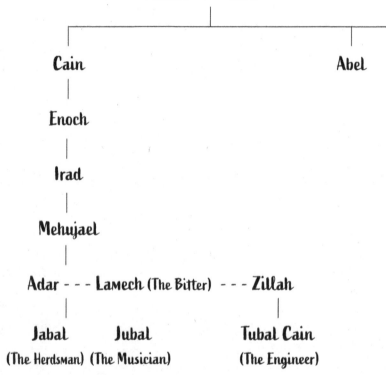

Adam - - - Eve

Cain                                              Abel

Enoch

Irad

Mehujael

Adar - - - Lamech (The Bitter) - - - Zillah

Jabal            Jubal                    Tubal Cain
(The Herdsman) (The Musician)      (The Engineer)

**Seth**
(The image of Adam)

**Enosh**
(At this time, people
begin to worship God)

**Kenan**

**Mehalalel**

**Jared**

**Enoch**
(Walked with God)

**Methuselah**

**Lamech** (The Good)

**Noah**

## CHAPTER 1

# Baby Noah

Farmer Lamech and his wife lived at a time when life was especially difficult for farmers. There was something wrong with the ground, and the weather didn't help either.

Every year, they would start work in the fields, getting them ready for sowing and planting, and every year Lamech would say to his wife, "Perhaps this year will be a good one," and she would reply, "Let's hope so, Lamech. Let's hope so."

But it didn't seem to work out like that. The hot sun baked the soil until it was as hard as bone and difficult to plough. Lamech seemed to be forever repairing his plough. When the rain came, it fell all at once, making everything so muddy that the oxen got stuck. When the wind blew, it knocked over all the corn that Lamech had looked after so carefully, and it shook all the fruit from the trees.

The weeds didn't worry a bit about the weather. They just kept growing stronger, and each year their prickles seemed to grow longer and sharper.

Farming seemed to be such a dreary business. Mr and Mrs Lamech worked tirelessly at spreading the muck and ploughing it in. Then they went up and down with the harrow until the soil was lovely and soft and smooth. Then it was time to sow their seeds.

Once the plants had begun to grow, they had to be hoed and weeded, and the birds and rabbits had to be kept away until the crop was ready to gather in.

Year after year at harvest time, it was disappointing to see what they had managed to grow. There was never quite enough.

Even the oxen seemed to struggle. They would look at one another and roll their eyes every time Lamech broke the plough. At the end of each day's work, they would be glad to be taken out of their harness and led to their stall for a manger full of hay, a long drink of water, and a good night's rest.

Lamech knew very well why it was all like this. People had behaved so badly that God had arranged for the land to misbehave too. These were dark and troubled times. People were becoming wild, fighting and killing each other, stealing, and smashing things. It was not only a bad time to be a farmer; it was a bad time to be anyone.

All this made God really sad. He had originally made the world to be a special and beautiful place for people to live in. He had wanted them to love him, to love one another, and to look after the world that he had made for them, but everything was going terribly wrong.

God realized that if he left things as they were, the whole world would be completely wrecked, and all the people would be dead, so he started looking round for someone he could trust. He decided that things were so bad he would have to destroy everything and start all over again with a family that was good, and really loved him; a family that would know how to care for the world he had given them.

Then something wonderful happened: Mrs Lamech had a baby boy.

When he was born, Mr and Mrs Lamech were filled with joy and hope. They somehow knew that he was going to be particularly special. It helped them to think of good times to come, and not to be so worried about all the horrible things that were going on around them. They knew that this little baby was a gift from God, and they were so thankful.

They decided to call him Noah, which in their language meant "comfort".

"God is going to use this little child to bring us comfort," said Lamech. "He will bring us rest from this constant hard work and disappointment."

Mrs Lamech looked down into the face of the little child cradled in her arms.

"Yes, you will, won't you, my little man. You will bring us comfort," she said, and little Noah looked up at her and said, "ggrrble wrrble," which she took to mean "You just wait and see."

And she was right. God did use Noah to bring comfort to a very uncomfortable world, but as usual with God, things didn't turn out quite as anybody had expected.

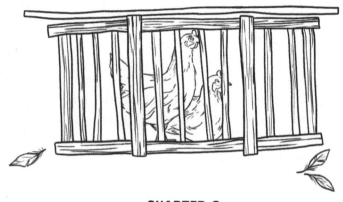

## CHAPTER 2

# Noah Grows Up

As little Noah got bigger and stronger, he helped his father on the farm. He learned how to grow things and how to look after the animals. His father taught him how to make things out of wood and metal.

They made houses for all the farm animals – big strong sheds for the bigger animals, and little shelters for the smaller ones. Then there were little houses on wheels where the chickens could lay their eggs and roost at night.

Noah had some creatures of his own, of course. Best of all he loved his doves. They were gentle and beautiful, with smooth, shiny white feathers and big dark eyes. He loved their soft comforting call, and he loved to see them flying white against the clear blue sky.

Noah had made a particularly beautiful house for his doves. It had six sides and a pretty roof that finished at the top with a little decorative spike. There were doors in the sides, each with its own perch for the doves to land on.

As Noah grew into manhood, he took more and more responsibility for the farm. His father, Lamech, was getting older. He was unable to manage a lot of the tasks that had to be done.

Eventually, Noah took over the running of the whole farm. It was good for him to be in charge of everything. He learned a lot and was very busy, but however much Noah had to do, and however busy he was, he always made time to be quiet with God. He made a habit of going for a long walk every day. That way he could talk to God and learn to listen to his voice.

One day as he was walking, Noah noticed a curled-up leaf being blown along on the surface of a puddle. It looked like a ship on the sea. It even made its own little wave that spread out behind it on the water as it scudded along. He stood and watched it for a few moments as it was blown to and fro.

Then he thought he heard God say something like, "Noah, there is a special job that I want you to do for me."

Noah replied, "I will do whatever you want, Lord."

He spoke into the air, but he knew that God could hear everything and would understand what he meant.

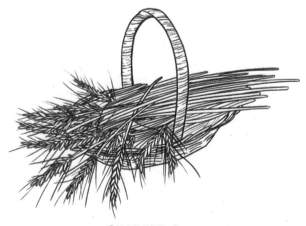

**CHAPTER 3**

# Team Noah

God found a good wife for Noah. She loved God too. She told Noah that she would support and help him, whatever he felt God was saying to him.

Over the next few years, God gave Noah and his wife three lovely strong boys. Their names were Shem, Ham, and Japheth.

Noah loved his boys. He made toys for them to play with and model boats to sail on the pond and in the bath. He made a lovely pram that was perfect for wheeling the youngest one along with him during his long walks. It looked a bit like a boat, and it had a flag with a picture of a dove on it.

Sometimes Noah would gather all three boys up into his arms and squeeze them.

"This is my lovely ham sandwich," he would say,

rubbing his beard into their faces. They would giggle and squeal. The littlest one would say, "ggrrble wrrble," and everybody knows what that means!

When it came to bedtime, Mr and Mrs Noah had a special song that they would sing to help the boys go to sleep:

> *"The Lord is good.*
> *His faithfulness reaches to the heavens.*
> *The Lord is good.*
> *His love endures for ever."*

It always worked. Mrs Noah would start, and Noah would join in with the bass line. By the time they had repeated the song five or six times, all their boys were snoring away happily.

As they grew older, Noah's three sons learned to make things for themselves with bits of wood and metal. Noah taught them how to use tools, and if he was too busy, they could always ask Grandad Lamech to help them.

It wasn't long before they were all big enough and clever enough to be a great help around the farm. Noah and his boys made a really good team. They loved working with their dad and their Grandad Lamech.

By and by, the boys grew into big, strong men. God found a lovely wife for each of them. These girls were so happy to be a part of Noah's family team, away from the madness and violence of the world that they had grown up in. Here in Noah's family it was different. There was no violence, lying, or bad language; here they were loved and respected. They felt safe.

The girls all joined in with the work on the farm and around the house. They helped with the crops and caring for the animals. They helped with the cooking and the gardening. Things had never been in such good shape.

Old Lamech watched as they all worked together so cheerfully. He smiled and remembered the words that had been spoken when Noah was a little baby, and of the name that they had given him.

*He has brought us comfort,* he thought, and he was full of thankfulness to God, but there was much more to come.

## CHAPTER 4

# A Special Task for Team Noah

It was at this time, when things seemed to be working out so well on the family farm, that Noah felt God speaking to him in much more detail about what he wanted him to do. He was on one of his long, quiet, thoughtful walks, when he heard God speak.

"Noah," he heard him say, "I am so sad about the way that people in the world are behaving. They have become violent and cruel. They are destroying one another and wrecking the world that I have made for them."

"I know what you mean," replied Noah. "It troubles me terribly to see people behaving as they do. I can understand how it must upset you, Lord. I often wonder what will become of us all."

"Noah, I have a job for you and your family," continued God.

"Yes, Lord. I think I have heard you mention that before," answered Noah. "Tell me what you have in mind. I will do anything you say."

There was a long silence. Noah kept walking and listening. Then he felt God speaking again.

"What I am planning is to destroy all the Earth and its people in a great and catastrophic flood. Everything has got to go, so that I can start afresh."

Noah didn't know what to say, so he just kept on walking.

"I want you and your family to build an enormous boat. I am going to save you and your family, and lots of animals too."

Noah said nothing. He kept walking and listening.

"Then we can start all over again, and things will be new and different."

Noah carried on walking. He took a turn in the road, veering from his usual route to make his walk a few miles longer. He needed more time to think. First of all, he thought that this task would be too big for him, but then he began to think of how God might have been preparing him and his family over the years of his life. He thought of all that his father, Lamech, had taught him; how he had got used to supervising all the work on the farm; all the sheds that he and his boys had built together to house the animals; and how they had made plenty of toy boats to sail on the pond. He thought of his three strong boys, each with a lovely wife. His father, Lamech, was still alive to offer his advice and wisdom.

"You have given me a good team, Lord," he said at last, "but this would be a massive project. It's more than one family can do."

"Yes, it is," replied God, "but hey, Noah, don't forget – there's me too! I shall be with you all the way."

"Yes, of course, Lord. I'm sorry. I know that you are a faithful God. You can do anything. I know that you will not leave us to struggle on our own."

So Noah stopped worrying and began to listen more carefully to the details of the boat that God wanted him to build. It was to be 450 feet long – it would take a good stiff walk to get from one end to the other; and 75 feet wide – all eight of Noah's family standing side by side and holding hands would only reach half way across. It would stand 50 feet high – much higher than all the family standing on one another's shoulders. In other words, it was going to be HUGE.

When he got back to the farm, Noah wrote down all the details that God had shown him. He didn't want to forget anything.

The next morning, Noah called all the family together for a team meeting. He wanted to tell them all about what he had heard.

Mrs Noah's kitchen was the hub of the farm. That's where plans were made. So that is where everybody gathered that morning. Grandad Lamech was already there, of course, sitting comfortably by the warm stove sipping from a mug of sweet mint tea.

They all sat round the big kitchen table. Mrs Noah poured out the tea; a plate of oatcakes sat in the middle of the table. Noah took out the instructions he had written down.

"My dears," he began, "I have told you that God has a special job for us all to do. Well, now I think I know a little bit more about what he wants."

Noah helped himself to an oatcake and dipped it in his tea. He bit off the soft piece, and with his mouth full of soggy oatcake, he continued his address to the assembled family team.

"God is really upset about all the violence and evil in the world. He thinks that if things carry on as they are, everything will be destroyed. He says that if the violence and evil continue, there will be no one left. He wants to start all over again. He is planning to send a catastrophic flood upon the Earth."

Everyone was shocked. Japheth choked on the oatcake he was eating. The crumbs scattered all over the table.

"A flood!" he exclaimed, sweeping up the crumbs with his sleeve. "But I can't even swim!"

"Let me finish," continued Noah. "You won't need swimming lessons, my boy, because we are all going to build a boat – a big boat. Actually, it's going to be a really big boat. It will be HUGE!"

"That's brilliant," said Shem. "I've always wanted to build a big boat."

"This is going to be *really* big," answered Noah, "450 feet long and 75 feet wide."

"Wow," said Ham. "That is big. That's MASSIVE!"

"It will take all of us to do the work, and anyone else that wants to join us. There will be places for all the animals and birds that God wants us to save. We will stock the boat with food for ourselves and for the animals so that we can ride out the storm. Then God will start again with this family and with the animals that we take with us."

There was a long silence while everybody tried to take in what Noah had told them. Japheth was the first to speak.

"Crumbs!" he said. Grandad Lamech laughed, but no one else noticed anything funny. They were all too busy thinking. Then Shem spoke up.

"Dad," he said thoughtfully, "I think you're right. It sounds like a crazy scheme, but I have a feeling that this really is God speaking. There is no other way out of the mess that we are all in. Let's go for it."

"I agree," added Ham. "We are used to working together as a family. You can't expect to do this on your own. We will throw our weight in behind you."

"Me too," said Japheth. "It will be good fun."

"And I will help where I can," said Lamech, "though I am not as strong as I once was."

Mrs Noah slipped her hand into Noah's. They exchanged a thankful glance.

"Thank God for all of you," said Noah. "Let's remember that the Lord himself will be with us throughout this whole adventure. That's what he has promised."

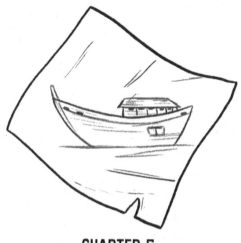

CHAPTER 5

# Designing the Big Boat

It meant a lot to Noah that his family were going to support him in this massive project.

Over the next few weeks, they found themselves talking about the design of the boat. They stood around in the yard and drew out their ideas in the sand. All this time, Noah was making time to be alone with God. He was trying to listen carefully for the important details. He even started to take something to write with on his long walks. He didn't want to miss anything that God wanted him to include in the design.

Noah tried to tell some of the people who lived around them about what God had asked him to do. They just laughed at him. So, he was very thankful for his family. It was a comfort to him that they took him seriously and trusted that he was really hearing God.

Shem was sent off on a journey to the coast to talk to people who built boats there. After some months, he returned with lots of helpful ideas and drawings. Then he suggested that they should build a model.

"If we make it to scale," said Shem, "we can see how everything will fit, and we can try it out on the farm pond. That's what boat-builders would do."

Everybody agreed that this was a brilliant idea. At first they thought that they would make the model ten times smaller than the real thing, but they soon realized that even then it would be the size of a large house. They eventually settled for making it one hundred times smaller than life size. That would be something like the size of Mrs Noah's kitchen table. It would be much more manageable, and anyway, they didn't want to waste too much time and effort on a model.

So they all set to work in the farm workshop, preparing the pieces of wood that they would need for the model. Noah let Shem take charge of this operation. Noah was pleased to see how good he was at organizing everything.

Noah explained some of the details that he felt God had shown him. The ship was to have three decks and some sort of opening all the way along the top.

"That would be so that everyone inside could get some air," said Ham.

"And we will need plenty of fresh rainwater for drinking and cooking," added Mrs Noah.

"Water for the animals too, of course," said Noah.

They realized that the boat would have to be strong enough to withstand some very rough seas, and it would have to be designed in such a way that it would keep its nose into the wind. Otherwise it would be a very uncomfortable ride for everyone inside and they would run the risk of being overturned by the waves.

Noah wanted to have a room high up in the roof from which they could look out. Someone suggested that Mrs Noah's kitchen should be up there, so they would all have somewhere to gather. Everyone agreed that it would be important to have Mrs Noah's kitchen on the boat.

So the model took shape. It was big enough that they could sort out problems as they arose, but it was small enough that any changes could be made quickly and easily.

When it was finished, Noah said that it should be painted all over with pitch to keep it watertight. That's what God wanted for the real thing. Painting with pitch is a messy business. Pitch is black sticky stuff, and it has to be painted on while it is hot. When that was done, and the pitch was dry, they were ready to try the model on the pond.

They filled the bottom of the boat with stones to keep it steady. They then loaded each deck with sand to represent the weight of the creatures and all their food.

Everybody gathered at the pond for the launch of their miniature ship. It stood bravely waiting at the edge of the water. Mrs Noah said that they should give it a name.

"Of course, my dear," answered Noah. "But we must first make sure that it floats nicely."

With that, they all gathered round the model and eased it out onto the water. It rode steadily out into the middle of the pond, perfectly upright. Everybody clapped.

"Now let's give it some waves," said Noah. A large log lay nearby. Shem and Ham managed to lift it between them. They threw it into the pond with an enormous splash. It sent a series of waves across the water, which set the boat bobbing and rocking, but it wasn't troubled.

"That's splendid!" said Noah. He had a long pole in his hand. He pushed at the top of the boat, to see if he could overturn it, but it just settled back into its upright position. It looked firm and secure and steady.

"Well done, everybody," said Noah. "She's looking strong and stable. We won't be able to test the real thing like this. She is going to have to be right first time."

So they spent the rest of that day testing the little boat for all sorts of possible troubles. They threw water at it. They pushed it and shoved it. They tipped it forwards and backwards and sideways. But the little model boat remained steadfastly floating the right way up. Japheth wanted to try to ride on it, but Shem wouldn't let him.

At the end of the day, the whole team gathered in Mrs Noah's kitchen.

"So how about a name for our boat?" said Mrs Noah.

There followed a long and animated conversation about what the boat should be called. Old Grandad Lamech wanted to call it "The Good Ship Comfort". Mrs Noah wanted to call it "Hope". Japheth wanted to call it "The Skylark". Shem thought that he was being silly again and said that he thought there were more important things to think about.

"You are right, my boy," said Noah. "There are many years of hard work ahead of us. Let's just call it an 'ark' for the moment, because that's what it is. We'll have plenty of time to think of a proper name later."

## CHAPTER 6

# Building the Ark

Now that they knew that their design was going to work, they started on the task of building the real thing. First they had to mark it out full-size on the ground. For this they needed a flat piece of land that was not too far from the house and workshop. Once they had chosen a suitable place, they harnessed up the oxen to a heavy harrow, and took them up and down to clear the weeds and large stones.

Next, they stretched a rope to mark the centre line of the great boat. Then, with a length of cord and a big wooden triangle, they set out the whole shape of the ark on the ground. They hammered in wooden pegs at every point where a cross-frame would need to stand.

Once it was all marked out, everyone began to realize what an absolutely massive project they had taken on.

So began a long chapter in the history of the Noah family, which afterwards they called "the building years".

They had to chop and cart big logs from the surrounding woodland. The wood had to be cut and shaped carefully, and then fitted together to make the frame of the ark. Very slowly over these building years, the enormous frame of the boat took shape. It looked like the skeleton of a huge sea creature.

The two younger boys were very clever and good at inventing things. They were sure that the water that came rushing down the hills behind the farm could be used to power a saw. They had heard of people who ground their corn into flour that way, so they made a big wooden wheel with paddles that turned in the flowing water. This they joined by a series of cogs and wheels to a nodding arm like a great see-saw. To this they fixed a frame with sharp saw blades. It meant that they could put a whole log into this machine and leave it to turn a big lump of wood into boards. They had to tinker with it and improve it over the years, but when they had finally got it working nicely, it saved them a lot of time and effort.

Once the frame of the ark was complete, the boards had to be fixed to the sides. Each day, the team did a little more, and each year they could see what had been achieved.

Over these building years, old Lamech gradually grew weaker and less able to work. When he found that he couldn't walk very far from the house, the boys made him a chair with wheels. Each day, someone would wheel him out to see how the work was progressing. Even though he could no longer saw wood or bang in nails, he was still able to give advice on how to do things. He understood the reasons for this work, so his daily visits were always an encouragement to those who were working on the boat.

You could often hear someone say something like, "Oops! I had better tidy up this mess before Grandad Lamech sees it" or "I will just try to get this finished before Grandad comes round." So although Grandad Lamech wasn't very good at moving himself, he somehow helped to keep the work on the ark moving along steadily.

Everybody liked to hear him say, "My, that's a good job you're doing there!" or "Goodness me, that's come a long way since I last saw it!"

About five years before the ark was finished, old man Lamech died. Noah and the rest of the family were very sad to lose him, but they were comforted to think that he had seen the great ship take shape.

Although they were all so busy building the ark, as well as looking after everything on the farm, Noah still made sure that he took some time each day to be quiet with God, speaking to him and learning to listen.

As the building work progressed, the people who lived around them took an interest in what was happening. They thought that Noah and his family were crazy.

Noah tried to talk to them. He told them that God was sad at the way things were turning out in the world, but they just laughed at him. He wanted them to say sorry to God for the bad things that were going on. He told them that God would forgive them and that there would be plenty of room in the ark, but they said, "Noah, you are crazy. We have lived here for generations, and there has never been a flood before."

Some people thought that what Noah was saying was just a clever way of getting more people to help with the building work.

"We are far too busy," they said. "There are parties to organize and weddings to attend. We haven't got time to think about all this nonsense. Get a life, Noah!"

There were others who were just not interested in what Noah was saying.

"He is a nice enough fellow," they said, "but we see things differently." So they carried on life as normal, and tried to get what they could for themselves and their families.

It took many years of hard work, an awful lot of wood, and thousands of nails, but finally the day came when the great wooden ship was complete. Then it had to be painted all over with black pitch.

Pitch comes out of the ground in big hard lumps, a bit like hard black toffee. Noah and the team had to melt it before they could paint it onto the sides of the ark.

Noah set up a big iron tub over a fire to melt the pitch, while the rest of the team set about the messiest of jobs. Everyone wore their oldest clothes. They filled their buckets from Noah's big tub and then painted the ark all over, inside and out.

It wasn't just the ark that turned black; it was the family too. However hard they tried to keep clean, they all ended the day with black smudges everywhere. It took weeks to complete this job. The whole family was so relieved when it was all done that they gathered in Mrs Noah's kitchen for a celebratory meal. Everybody helped with the preparations. They even scrubbed the black footprints off the floor.

## CHAPTER 7

# The Ark

At last the ark was complete. It stood there – big and black and shiny.

Noah and his family decided to have a well-deserved day off. They set off for a picnic in the hills, just to get away from it all and have a rest.

Mrs Noah's cat, Clysmic, thought that she would have an adventure too, so she set about the task of exploring the ark while it was empty and the family were away.

High up on one side was the door. It was big enough for a cart to drive through. The team had piled up rocks, stones, and soil very carefully to make a firm, sloping road up to the open door, so that people, animals, and the cart could get in and out easily.

Clysmic trotted boldly up this sloping road and in through the door. She found herself on the top floor, or deck. Here it was light and airy, because high up in the roof above was an air vent with shutters. This stretched all the way from one end of the boat to the other. She sniffed the fresh air.

As far as she could see in every direction, there were cages and pens for the animals and birds to live in. Today it was all still and silent. What she didn't know was that the whole place would soon be filled with the constant noise of birds and animals.

In the middle of this top deck were the rooms (or cabins) for Noah and his family to live in. Clysmic climbed the staircase that led from the lower cabins to the higher ones. She was not able look into these rooms, but she sniffed at the gap below the doors and quickly worked out which one belonged to Mr and Mrs Noah. She made a mental note that this was where to come and miaow if she ever got fed up in the middle of the night.

She carried on beyond the cabins, up the stairs, and through the hatchway into Mrs Noah's kitchen/lookout. This was set high up in the middle of the roof. Here there was a stove in one corner for cooking, with a chimney pipe going up through the roof.

*This is going to make a nice place for a snooze,* she thought.

On each side of the room were windows with wooden shutters. She jumped up to a windowsill and looked out over the surrounding countryside.

Noah's farm looked so small, and such a long way down. It made her feel a bit dizzy, so she quickly jumped down again.

At each end of the kitchen, there was a door that opened onto a covered balcony. She could see that this would make another good place for a quiet nap, even when it was raining.

Going back down the stairs to the top deck, and not far from the big door, there was a wide slope that took her down to the next level. Here it was a bit gloomier, but there were vents all along that brought in the light and she could smell the air from the top deck even though everything smelled so strongly of pitch. This floor was also full of animal cages and pens. She sensed that, in time, it would make good mouse-hunting country.

Then she made her way down to the lowest deck, where the bigger animals would be living, and the ones that prefer the dark. Here too were rooms for storing barrels and boxes of food. All the heavier things would be down here, to help keep the boat steady. This also looked like good hunting ground.

Down below this was the bottom deck. Here the humans would have to mind their heads because of the low ceiling. These were the bilges. They were packed with lots of stones, rocks, and pebbles. This heavy ballast would help to keep the whole ship the right way up, and give a much more comfortable ride in rough weather. This bottom deck was of no great interest to Clysmic.

On each deck there were water tanks. These were fed by a system of pipes from the roof. They would supply clean water for the animals and birds.

Clysmic worked her way back the way she had come, through the big doorway and down the sloping road. Her mind was elsewhere. She had already decided that she would find a nice little patch of warm sunshine somewhere, where she could settle down and snooze until the family returned.

Later that afternoon, everybody arrived back at the farmhouse. The women went into the house, but Noah and his boys stood together looking up at the great ship. It was enormous – very long and very wide, the sides bulging and curving like a great big black cow, sitting on the grass.

The front end (or bow) of the ark was sort of pointed, not as sharply as the beak of a bird, but more like the nose of a beaver. At the back end (or stern), there was a fixed rudder, then another on each side, sticking out a little toward the stern. This was to keep the whole ship pointing into the wind, so that it would stay steady in rough weather.

They stepped back a little further and looked up. They could just about see the kitchen, high up in the middle of the roof. It looked surprisingly small compared to the great big ark. The roof was made of thick animal skins, all stitched together and fastened to the roof timbers to make a strong and waterproof covering.

As for the matter of the ship's name, nobody had ever mentioned it again. There was nothing painted in fancy letters on the bow. It had been called an ark for so many years that everyone knew it as "The Ark" with capital letters. Some people called it "Noah's Ark", but Noah knew that it was really God's Ark, specially designed by him, and built by Noah and his family, with strength and wisdom supplied by God.

## CHAPTER 8

# The Animals

Team Noah had finished all the main work of building, but there was still a lot to do, making all the cages and pens for the animals. Then there were all the fiddly bits, like putting a smooth handrail on the stairs, and getting all the doors and shutters to fit nicely.

It was at this time that the animals began to arrive. Just as God gives the swallow the ability to return each summer to the same nesting place from half way round the world, so he put a powerful thought into the minds of all the creatures that they must make their way to Noah. It was like an inner urge that they could not resist.

As they arrived, each little group of animals was cared for on the farm until things were ready for them in the Ark. Many of these creatures were really wild, but God gave them a trust for this special family. The fast animals like the deer and the hares did not run away. The fierce animals like the lions and the bears did not show their teeth. None of them were afraid. They allowed themselves to be taken in and made comfortable in their new homes.

This growing family of animals made Noah realize that the time was getting near when God would send the flood that he had promised. It made the team press on even more urgently with all the tasks that had to be completed. Time was running out. There was still so much to be done.

It was during these last few years that the crops on the farm were really blessed. Never before had Noah seen harvests like these.

*If only my old dad could have seen this*, he thought.

This time of plenty meant that they could begin to fill the big store-rooms on the Ark with corn and nuts, and fodder for the animals. Wonderful cartloads of sweet-smelling hay were trundled through the great door of the Ark. It was all stacked away on the lower decks to feed the grass-eating animals. Straw for bedding was carted too. Gradually, the overwhelming smell of pitch was being softened by the fragrance of the hay, straw, and grain.

As Noah sensed that the time for the flood was drawing near, he began to select the animals that would join them in the Ark. He chose a healthy young pair of every creature – one male and one female. He made sure that the fiercer animals were young enough and small enough to be easy to handle during the voyage. They would have plenty of time to grow big and strong later.

Then, for every kind that was good for food, he took seven animals, just as God had told him. That would mean that they would have enough for the family and the meat-eating animals during the voyage, and plenty left over to start a new farm and wildlife once the flood was over.

On the topmost deck, he put all the creatures that liked to see the light. Here were many of the birds in their big wire cages. This was also where the chickens, ducks, and geese lived, which would provide the family with both eggs and meat. And this is where Noah put his doves, in a specially built cage next to his cabin.

On the lower decks were the larger grass-eating animals. The goats, cows, and sheep would provide the family with milk, cheese, and meat.

As more and more of the cages and pens filled up with creatures, so the noise on the Ark grew louder, and the smells grew stronger.

## CHAPTER 9

# The Flood Begins

Seven days before the flood arrived, God spoke to Noah, and Noah heard him very clearly. He knew that he had just a week to get his family into the Ark before the flood came. Most of the animals were comfortably housed in their quarters, so this last week was spent getting all the things into the Ark that the family would need.

They loaded the farm cart with tables and chairs, beds, carpets, pots, dishes, knives, forks, spoons, ladles, saucepans, and so on and so on. Mr and Mrs Noah had prepared lots of plants, and boxes and barrels of seeds, so that they could get things growing again once the flood was over.

After their last journey with the cart, they stowed it away in the Ark and put the oxen in their stall. The cart and oxen would be needed at the other end of the voyage.

These were anxious days for Noah. He kept looking up at the sky. Heavy dark clouds were building up, and he could hear thunder rumbling in the distance. On the morning of the final day, the sky was blacker than ever, and the thunder was getting closer. The whole family gathered in Mrs Noah's kitchen and Noah spoke to them very seriously.

"I want everyone to get into the Ark," he said, "and once inside, it is very important that no one leaves." Noah usually spoke with a kind and gentle voice, but today he sounded more like a bossy schoolteacher. He seemed to be very edgy. "Let's gather inside the door as soon as we can."

Noah went through the house and workshop and gathered up a few last bits that might come in useful. As he strode purposefully up the slope into the Ark, he looked up again at the darkening sky. He went through the great door into the top deck, the scent of sweet fresh hay and straw heavy in the air. He could tell that the animals were more restless than usual. They too could sense the approaching storm.

The family was waiting for him inside the door, just as he had told them to.

"OK. Have we got everyone?" asked Noah.

"Shem?"

"Yes, Dad – and Mrs Shem."

"That's good," said Noah. "Have we got Ham?"

"Yes, I'm here," said Ham.

"And so am I," said Mrs Ham.

"What about Japheth? I can't see him. Where's that boy got to?"

"He is here, Noah. Don't worry," answered Mrs Japheth, "and I am too."

"Thank God," said Noah. "Now, where's Mrs Noah? Has anyone seen Mrs Noah?"

"She's not here," said Shem. "Perhaps she's in the kitchen."

"Go and look, son. Be quick," said Noah urgently.

Shem ran up the stairs, two at a time. He disappeared through the hatchway into the roof-kitchen. Soon he was back again.

"She's not there, Dad," said Shem.

"Has anyone seen her?" asked Noah. They all looked blankly at him. Ham shrugged his shoulders.

"Right then, I'm going back to the house. No one else is to leave the Ark. Is that clear?" They all nodded.

"Make a search of the whole boat. I will be back as soon as I can."

With that, Noah ran back down the slope and across to the house, anxiously glancing up at the clouds.

"Are you there, Mrs Noah?" he shouted as he burst through the door. He heard a faint reply.

"I'm in the larder, Noah. I won't be long." Noah pushed open the larder door and almost knocked Mrs Noah over. She was standing on a stool with a basket in her hand, trying to get the cat down from the top shelf.

"She won't come down, Noah. Give me a hand."

"We need to go, my dear," said Noah. "There's no time for this."

"But we shall need the cat on the Ark."

"We already have two," answered Noah.

"That's different," said Mrs Noah defiantly. "I'm pretty sure we've got more than two mice on that boat."

"Oh, all right; I take your point," replied Noah, "but let's be quick about it."

Mrs Noah stepped down, and Noah climbed up on the stool. He took the cat firmly, but gently, into his arms. He knew that he must not hurry when handling animals. It only causes trouble. He placed the cat gently into the basket, and Mrs Noah fastened the lid.

"There you are Clysmic," she said. "We will soon find a new home for you."

"Come on, my dear. We must get into the Ark," said Noah, taking the basket. "I don't think we have much time."

The two of them walked arm in arm out of the house. A blustery wind had picked up. It tugged at their clothes. Noah looked up at the sky. There was a great flash of lightning followed quickly by a loud crack of thunder.

"Goodness me!" said Mrs Noah. "Not a moment too soon!" They hurried up the slope toward the great door of the Ark, the wind buffeting them all the way. It was a struggle to stay on their feet.

Suddenly there was a squall of rain and a strong gust of wind. The great wooden door of the Ark, which had been pegged open for months, rattled and shook violently. Mr and Mrs Noah hurried through the doorway into the shelter of the Ark. Immediately the door broke free from its peg. It swung wildly back and forth. Then came an enormous burst of wind. The door slammed shut with a loud crash and stuck fast. It was firmly closed. There was no going back. All the family came running.

"Thank God you two are here, and safely inside," puffed Shem.

Another flash of lightning lit up the sky for a split second, then came a crash of thunder so mighty that the big ship trembled. All the creatures bellowed and barked and roared. Then came the rain. It drummed upon the thick leather roof-covering, quietly at first, but the noise gradually increased until it was a steady roar.

"This is it!" shouted Noah over the noise. "We will have to get used to this din."

## CHAPTER 10

# Noah's Log

That night, as all Noah's family settled into their cabins, Mr and Mrs Noah went up the stairs by the light of an oil lamp and slipped into theirs. Mrs Noah had already made everything comfortable.

They closed the door behind them and Noah placed the lamp on the stand at his side of the bed.

"It is so peaceful in here," said Mrs Noah, "away from all the noise of the animals, and the drumming of the rain."

They sat on the bed together and offered a prayer of thanks to God, grateful to be in the shelter of the Ark with all that water outside. They quickly changed into their nightclothes. Before getting into bed, Mrs Noah sat at her dressing table. She let her hair down and reached for her comb.

"Oh dear, Noah," she said, "I've left my comb behind. All that fuss with the cat must have distracted me."

"Don't you worry, my dear," replied Noah. "You get some sleep. We can soon make you a new comb in the morning."

Mrs Noah wriggled down into the bed. It had been an exhausting day. Soon she was snoring away, fast asleep.

Noah sat up in the bed and took a book from under the pillow. He stuffed the pillow behind his back and made himself comfortable. He uncorked a new bottle of ink and opened the book to the first page. He dipped his pen into the bottle, and taking great care not to spill any ink on the bedclothes, he wrote in big letters across the page, "NOAH'S LOG". Then he turned to the next page and wrote the date at the top.

Noah was 600 years old when the flood came, so he counted the date from his birthday. He wrote, "Month two, day seventeen." Then, before he wrote his entry for the first day in the Ark, he made a note of the weather: "blustery, thundery, and very wet". He left a bit of a space before he wrote:

> Everybody safely inside the Ark, thank the Lord. We are all in good spirits.
> The door is shut fast. Water collection system working well.

Then, before he settled down for the night, Noah took out his pocketknife and cut a little mark on the wooden wall of the cabin.

"This is the first day of our voyage," he said to himself. "I must keep a careful record."

## CHAPTER 11

# Afloat at Last

The next morning, all the crew of the Ark met for breakfast in Mrs Noah's kitchen perched high up in the roof. Noah tried opening one of the shutters to look out, but it was blowing and raining so hard that it was impossible to see very far. One thing was very clear, however: there was water everywhere.

Still the great ship remained unmoved. It sat firmly in its cradle between two great banks of earth and stone.

The next night, Noah was fast asleep when he had a dream. He was high up in a tree, gathering apples. The wind was blowing, and the tree was swaying from side to side. He tried to hang on tightly to a branch, but suddenly he lost his grip on the basket of apples and it fell to the ground. At that moment he woke up, just as his boots fell from the wooden chest beside his bed and tumbled to the floor of the cabin.

Something strange was going on. Mrs Noah woke up too.

"What's happening?" she asked sleepily.

"I think..." replied Noah. "I think we are afloat, but we seem to be the right way up, so that's something to be thankful for."

He lit the oil lamp and shuffled unsteadily across to the cabin door. He made his way down the steps to the deck below. He was so thankful for the strong smooth handrail to guide him down.

The rain was still drumming on the roof and the animals were fidgeting and muttering to one another, unaccustomed to this new movement, but all seemed to be well.

"Dad, is that you?" Seth's voice came out of the darkness.

"We're afloat, my boy."

A light appeared from the cabins above them, and then another.

"Is everything OK?" The lamps came down to floor level and then came together. They could all see one another's faces. They were grinning.

"We're afloat at last."

"Thank God," said Noah, "and everything seems to be fine."

"Noah?" Mrs Noah's voice came from above them.

"It's all right, my dear. All is well."

"Thank you, Lord," said Mrs Noah quietly. "Thank you. Thank you."

"Let's get back to bed, boys," said Noah. "We will check for leaks in the morning. We will probably have to get the pumps into action."

Noah and the boys made their way back up the stairs to their cabins, but Mr and Mrs Noah couldn't get back to sleep. They got dressed and went up to Mrs Noah's kitchen. Noah lit the stove and brewed a pot of sweet mint tea. Clysmic the cat came and curled up by the warm stove. Mr and Mrs Noah sipped their tea and dozed in their chairs until the grey light of dawn could be seen through the cracks in the window shutters.

Gradually the rest of the family appeared in the kitchen. They were all a bit sleepy. Nobody had slept very well, but they were so very thankful that the great Ark was afloat with its precious cargo, and everything seemed to be working.

Breakfast was a rather thoughtful meal that morning. Most of the family were feeling excited, some a bit nervous, but they were all glad that their great adventure had begun at last. One or two were feeling a bit sick with the movement of the boat.

Once all the feeding of the animals was done that morning, Noah and the boys took their lamps down into the bilges below the bottom deck, just to see how much water had come in. Then everyone took turns to work the pumps, until the levels had gone right down. They knew that, as time went on, the water would cause the wood to swell, and any gaps between the boards would close. The whole ship would become more watertight.

That night, after cutting another mark on his cabin wall, Noah wrote another page in his log:

> Month two. Day eighteen. Weather – heavy rain and windy.
>
> We are all afloat at last. All is well. Ark riding nicely on the water. We are all feeling a little bit queasy, but nobody has actually been sick. It's taking a while to get used to decks that move.
>
> The creatures have been restless. Some of the larger animals find it more comfortable to sit rather than stand.

Over the next days and weeks, the crew of the great Ark got used to their daily routine. Breakfast was taken together up in Mrs Noah's kitchen. Then there were all the animals to care for, all needing food and water, and some needing fresh straw for their bedding. Usually everyone would have to take their turn on the pumps, and then there might be a bit of repair work to the boat itself, or to some of the cages or animal pens. One of the rooms on the top deck had been fitted out as a workshop with all the tools and equipment to keep the Ark shipshape.

Each evening, one of the team had the job of preparing supper. So, once the day had come to an end, and the last of the grey and stormy light had faded away, they lit their oil lamps and everyone gathered in the kitchen to enjoy a meal and catch up on the events of the day. They would talk about which animals had been born, which birds had laid eggs, and which creatures looked as though they might be needing a bit of extra special care. They talked about the boat and how much water was in the bilges, and they made a list of repairs or alterations that were needed.

Once the meal was over, it was time for washing the dishes. That was the easiest task of all. They gathered the pots and pans, and dishes and spoons into a big basket, and tied it to the railings outside in the rain. By the morning everything would be washed clean.

## CHAPTER 12

# Sunshine

Each evening, when Noah came to make up his log, there was one line that troubled him. The date was different each day, of course, and the things that happened varied from day to day, but one thing was always the same: the weather. Noah didn't like to write the same words over and over again, so he tried to be a little bit creative. He remembered a saying that his old dad, Lamech, would often re-peat: "Variety is the spice of life." So every day, he sat and chewed the end of his pen for a while, while he thought of a different way of saying "heavy rain". He tried "water streaming from the heavens", "rain drumming on the roof all day", "constant rain again", "steady downpour", and so on. Once or twice, he was tempted to write, "chucking it down again", but he decided that it was not the way to be writing the log of God's special Ark. However, the fact of the matter was that every day the weather *was* the same!

Sometimes the constant rain and dark clouds made some of the crew feel a bit low. Even some of the animals were beginning to look sad. Only the ducks and geese, and other water birds, were happy with the way things were.

Sometimes the constant loud quacking of the ducks sounded as though they were laughing at everyone else. If anyone was feeling a bit down in the dumps, this only made things worse. Then one day, everything changed.

One morning, when Noah was in bed, he suddenly found himself wide awake. He sat up and listened. Something strange was going on, but he couldn't quite put his finger on what it was. It was still dark, so he listened carefully to all the noises in the Ark. He could hear the birds beginning to make their early-morning tweets and warbles, and there seemed to be the sound of the animals fidgeting and muttering to one another. He had not noticed that noise before. Something was different.

Then he realized what it was: the constant drumming of the rain on the roof-covering had stopped.

He slipped out of bed, wrapped his dressing gown around him, and quietly opened the cabin door. Outside the cabin was a different sort of light than usual. He looked up to the vents in the roof.

It was still not quite dawn, but the light that shone through them was no longer drab and grey. It was clean and clear and golden. It sparkled.

Noah crept upstairs to Mrs Noah's kitchen and opened one of the shutters. He could hardly believe his eyes. High up in the sky he could see some stars, and far away on the distant eastern horizon was a glowing patch of light. He put his elbows on the sill, thrust out his head, and took a big breath of the cool, clear morning air. It smelled wonderful and fresh and new.

Noah ran down the stairs to the cabins below and hammered on each door.

"Come on, everybody! Get up to the kitchen as soon as you can. The rain has stopped and the sun is about to rise."

One after another, the cabin doors opened.

"What's going on?" asked Shem.

"Noah, are you going crazy?" asked Mrs Noah crossly.

By this time, Noah was on his way up the stairs to the kitchen again. He shouted back at the top of his voice.

"It's stopped raining. Quickly, come and see!" Then he disappeared up into the kitchen.

One by one, he was joined by the other members of the family. One after another the shutters along the east-facing side of Mrs Noah's kitchen flew open. Then, as the sun began to appear over the far edge of the water, a great cheer went up from the Ark.

"Thank you, Lord!" said Mrs Noah. Then Mr Noah began to sing in his big bass voice:

> *"The Lord is good. His faithfulness reaches to the heavens."*

He sang quietly at first, then Mrs Noah joined in, then the rest of the family. It was a song that they knew well. Again and again they sang those words.

> *"The Lord is good.*
> *His faithfulness reaches to the heavens.*
> *The Lord is good.*
> *His love endures for ever."*

As the sun rose higher in the sky, the kitchen filled with light. Everybody started dancing. They joined hands around the table and danced and sang at the tops of their voices.

After some time, Noah sat down.

"I think that will do for now," he said breathlessly. "Let's get some working clothes on and get the chores done. I think this calls for a celebration. We will have a special supper this evening. Mrs Noah and I will prepare the food."

So that day, while the rest of the family did the feeding and watering of all the animals, Mr and Mrs Noah prepared the best meal that they could muster. There was roasted lamb with spicy sauce. Freshly baked bread and olive oil to dip it in. Lots of little dishes of roasted grain and nuts, olives, raisins, and dates. Then, to wash it all down, there was a big jug of mint tea sweetened with honey, and a jug of Noah's best wine.

The sea had been calm all day, so the Ark was hardly moving as they gathered in Mrs Noah's kitchen that evening. They all sat round the table, and Noah said a prayer of thanks just as the sun began to drop down toward the western horizon.

The whole crew was in good spirits as they shared that meal together. They all knew that there was still a long wait before they could again stand on dry ground, but it felt as if the most difficult bit was over.

There was, however, something that weighed upon Mrs Noah's mind as the food disappeared, and the plates emptied. Since it was no longer raining, who was going to do the washing up?

She need not have worried. A big tub of water was lifted onto the table, and they all washed the dishes together.

Later that evening, when everyone else had settled in their cabins, Noah reached for the ship's log and turned to a new page. He wrote the date at the top. It was the third month and the twenty-seventh day. Below the date, he drew a big round sun with a smiley face, and lots of rays coming from it like the legs of a spider. Underneath he wrote:

Blue sky and sunshine all day,
HALLELUJAH!

Today we woke early to the strange sound of no rain hammering down on the roof. No gurgling in the water pipes, only the calls of the awakening creatures.

From the kitchen lookout we could see stars for the first time since we set out, and there on the distant horizon a growing patch of light. The whole family watched as the sun rose into a cloudless sky. We all sang and danced.

We finished the day with a special meal to celebrate God's wonderful faithful love to us.

Food supplies lasting well. Everybody in high spirits.

Praise God.

## CHAPTER 13

# Back to Earth with a Bump

Having sunshine made an enormous difference to everyone on the Ark. People were singing and whistling as they went about their daily work. It wasn't just the humans. The birds were singing and whistling too. As soon as the light began to appear each morning through the open shutters in the roof, the songbirds would start. Then the cockerels and the less musical birds would join in. None of the crew had to be woken in the morning. The birds got them out of bed.

All the creatures had a sense that things were changing for the better. Babies began to arrive. The smaller animals were first – rabbits, squirrels, guinea pigs. The rats also rapidly increased in number, and as for the mice, they were impossible

60

to contain. They found their way into all the nooks and crannies of the boat, and made a nuisance of themselves amongst the food that was stored away for the other animals and humans. Clysmic was hard at work hunting every night.

The birds began to build nests. Noah's much-loved hen dove was sitting on eggs, and before long, two little chicks hatched. The hens wanted to sit on their eggs rather than let Noah's family take them for omelettes and cakes. So their numbers increased too.

As time went by, more and more of the creatures multiplied. Two became three or four, and seven became ten or fifteen or even twenty.

Only the larger animals remained as twos and sevens, because Noah had chosen small young ones to take with him on the Ark. The fiercer creatures, too, were not old enough or mature enough to have babies. Noah had chosen them very carefully, so that they would be easy to look after and handle while they were on the Ark. There would be plenty of time for them to grow big and have babies once the voyage was over.

So the daily work increased. Keeping this growing number of creatures clean, fed, and watered was an enormous task.

Then one morning, while everyone was hard at work, there was a loud crash, followed by a horrible grumbling, scraping noise. Everyone on two legs had a job to stay on their feet and everything with wings had to flap furiously to keep the right way up.

Noah was in the middle of feeding the chickens when the bump happened. He just about managed to stay on his feet, but the basket of corn that he was holding went flying, scattering corn all over the floor of the pen. This was great news for the chickens, who pecked it all up greedily, clucking excitedly as they did so.

Meanwhile, Mrs Noah lost two of her lovely stripy breakfast bowls, which slid off the table before she could catch them.

The great Ark had come to a standstill. It was no longer floating. It was stuck fast, jammed between two humps of ground in the mountains of Ararat.

That evening, Noah made up his log as usual. It was the seventh month and the seventeenth day:

> Weather fine and bright. The Ark has grounded and is at rest. It seems to be steady, and more or less upright. Everyone is cheerful, but we are all finding it strange to be walking on decks that are no longer moving.

He flicked back through his log to see how long it had been since the end of the heavy rain: almost four months.

The Ark was firmly stuck and would not be moving again. Noah and his family were going to have to stay where they were inside the boat until the deep water all round them went down and the ground had dried out enough for them to walk on it.

## CHAPTER 14

# Land in Sight

Now that the Ark was stuck and no longer floating, life became a bit strained for the crew of the great boat. With the number of animals on board increasing daily, things were getting crowded on the animal decks. The work became harder each day, with more for everybody to do, and less room to do it in.

When Noah's family looked out from their kitchen/lookout perched high up in the roof of the Ark, they could see nothing but water. Whichever way they looked, the view was the same. Sometimes it was sparkling blue in the sunshine, and other times it was rough and dark and stormy, but there was no denying the fact that there was an awful lot of water between them and the horizon. There was not a scrap of land to be seen anywhere.

One afternoon, Mrs Noah was pegging out the laundry on the balcony of the kitchen/lookout. After she had emptied her basket of clothes, she stood at the railings looking at the water that stretched far and wide in every direction.

Then she noticed something that she had not seen before. Far away in the distance was a patch of white foam. It looked as though waves were breaking on some rocks.

Noah was in the kitchen. It was his turn to prepare the meal that evening, and the smell of frying onions was drifting out of the open door.

"Noah," she called. "Come and have a look at this."

Noah pulled the pan off the heat and wiped his hands on his apron. He went out onto the balcony to join Mrs Noah under the flapping washing.

"Look," she said, pointing to the white patch in the distance. "What is going on there?"

Noah shielded his eyes with his hand and stared.

"I think," he said, "there is a little island appearing, and waves are breaking on the rocks. The water must be going down at last."

Over the next few days, more and more patches of land appeared. For Noah and the family, who had seen nothing but water for the past eight months, it was a wonderful relief to see these islands appearing all around them.

Noah took out his logbook to record this exciting development:

*Month ten. First day. Weather –
sunshine and showers. Little islands of
rock appearing all around us.*

Then a few days later:

*Month ten. Third day. Weather –
cloudy, with a few useful showers.*

*More land appearing all around us.
These little islands must be the tops
of the mountains.*

*Everybody feeling a lot more
cheerful, but so much work to do, with
ever-increasing numbers of creatures
on board.*

*Perhaps we should have carried a
small boat for exploration and maybe a
bit of fishing. No time to make one now.*

**CHAPTER 15**

# An Experiment with Birds

The crew of the Ark were so excited to see more and more land appearing. They were desperate to get out of the Ark, and to allow the animals to have more space. Noah felt this growing pressure from his family, but he remained firm.

"We must wait for the right time," he said as they all sat around the table one evening. "I know that we would all like to get out of the Ark, but if we get it wrong, we will lose some of the creatures. Let's wait for God to show us."

So they waited – and waited. From the kitchen/ lookout, they could see very little of what was happening on the ground; they could only see the things that were far away. Noah wanted to do something that would be a comfort for the family during this difficult waiting time. Then he had an idea.

"I am going to release one or two of the birds," he said to the family one evening. "They can always return to the Ark if they can't find enough food outside."

So the next morning the experiment began. Noah knew that ravens were strong birds and were good at surviving in wild and unfriendly places. He pulled on a strong pair of leather gloves. He took one of the big black birds, put it into a basket, and closed the lid. He carried the basket up the stairs to the kitchen. The rest of the crew joined him to see what would happen.

All the windows in the kitchen were wide open, with the shutters pegged back to let the light in. Noah took the bird from its basket and held it tight. He didn't want it flying around the kitchen, knocking things over and making a mess.

"Are we ready?" he asked. "Here goes!" With that he tossed the bird through the window. Everyone rushed to an open window to watch. The great bird spread its wings and flapped away with a loud croak. It dropped out of sight beyond the side of the Ark, and then they caught sight of it as it flew away low over the water.

They watched as it got smaller and smaller until it disappeared behind some rocks and was gone. The raven never returned to the Ark, but over the next few days the family did spot it flying to and fro.

"Let's try sending out a dove," said Noah. He went back downstairs to the dove's cage next to his cabin. He put a handful of corn into his pocket. Gently he gathered up his much-loved hen bird. Her feathers were soft and warm. If any of his birds would know the way back to the Ark, it would be this one. He slipped her inside his shirt and climbed back up the stairs to the kitchen.

Once there, he reached into his shirt and drew her out. Everyone watched as he lifted her in his cupped hands and tossed her gently out through the open window.

Up she flew into the clear blue sky. She circled a few times, and then away she went toward the distant islands. She looked so small in such a big sky. Noah wondered if she would be able to find her way back to the Ark, but as they all watched, they saw her turn. She flew in a great big circle right round the Ark. Then she headed back.

She landed on the roof of the kitchen. They could hear her little feet on the roof-covering. Noah took some corn from his pocket. He reached his hand up through the window, holding a little corn for the bird to see. Then he felt her feet on his hand, and her beak pecking up the corn. Very gently he drew her back into the Ark. He slipped her into his shirt again and took her downstairs to join her mate.

"You were very brave, my little beauty," he said. "We will try again in a week or so."

Seven days later Noah took his little white hen dove up to the kitchen for another flight outside the Ark. Once again everybody watched as she flew up into the sky, circled a few times, and then flew away from the Ark until she was nothing but a tiny white speck against the blue of the sky.

They all stood at the windows and watched, but she did not return. They waited, and Noah strained his eyes to see her. Once or twice he thought he could see a little white dot in the distance, but it was nothing.

One by one, the family left the kitchen to get on with the daily routine of cleaning out and feeding the animals. Last of all, Noah came away from the window, glancing over his shoulder as he did so.

Again and again that day, Noah climbed the stairs to the kitchen and looked out of the open window. He stood quietly and listened for the sound of his dove's little feet on the roof-covering, but he could hear nothing.

That evening, when all the family were gathered in the kitchen for supper, a wonderful thing happened. They all sat round the table and, as usual, they held hands while Noah led them in a prayer of thanks. It was during a moment of quiet after the prayer that they heard the gentle rustle of wings, and then the pitter-patter of the dove's feet.

Noah was at the window in a flash. He took a little corn in his hand and reached up through the open window. Soon he felt the bird step onto his fingers.

"There you are, my little beauty," he said as he carefully drew her in through the window and cradled her in his hands. "And what have you brought back for us?"

The whole family gathered round and stared with wonder at the little white bird that nestled comfortably in Noah's big rough hands. There in her beak was the first green thing that anyone had seen for almost a year – a freshly plucked leaf from an olive tree.

Later, when Noah was making up his log, he couldn't help smiling:

> Month eleven. Day eighteen. Weather – clear and bright.
> Today I sent out my best little hen dove. She was gone all day. I thought we had lost her, but in the evening she returned as we were all gathered for supper. I drew her into the Ark, and there in her beak was a fresh olive leaf.
> What wonders! Things are growing again. The Lord is good. His faithfulness reaches to the heavens.

Seven days later Noah was a little sadder when he wrote up his log:

> Month eleven. Day twenty-five.
> Weather – showery.

*This morning, I once again sent my little hen dove to spy out the surrounding land for us. She has not returned.*

*I think I know what she is up to. I know her well. She will be building a nest somewhere. Soon she will need a mate.*

Noah was sad to lose his best hen dove, but he knew that before long they would all be able to leave the Ark and make a new life upon the Earth.

## CHAPTER 16

# Fresh Air

The roof of the Ark was made from thick animal skins, carefully cut and stitched together, then nailed to the rafters. After all the weather that the Ark had been through since the voyage had begun, this covering had got a bit tatty. In some places it was beginning to leak. Everybody agreed that it was time to take it off.

Just a little more than a month after Noah had lost his much-loved dove, it was his six-hundred-and-first birthday.

"What shall we do to celebrate?" asked Mrs Noah.

"I think it's the perfect day to take off the roof-covering. That would be a fun job for us all to do," replied Noah.

So on the morning of Noah's birthday, after they had seen to the animals, the family got the ladders out and set to work.

It was a wonderful day for the family, but also for the animals. It meant that the Ark was filled with light and sweet-smelling fresh air. You could see all the creatures sniffing and blowing, enjoying all the new smells.

It also meant that they would get used to how things would be for them, once they left the shelter of the Ark. Noah said that it was "acclimatization". When they heard it, the boys looked at one another and shrugged.

"Happy birthday, Dad!" said Japheth.

Some of the pieces of roofing that came off were still in quite good condition. They would come in useful to repair the leaks that had appeared in the kitchen roof. A good roof would be needed on the kitchen for some time yet.

Once the covering had been removed, it was a great deal easier to see what they were doing when cleaning and feeding the animals. The whole boat smelled better too, and Mrs Noah, much to her surprise, found the comb that she thought she had left behind.

Without the covering they were able to have a good look at what was around them. Climbing up and looking over the sides of the Ark, they could easily see the ground below in much more detail. It was drying out nicely, and grass, trees, and bushes were beginning to grow again.

They knew that it wouldn't be very long now before they would be able to set foot on solid ground.

At the end of the day, the family made their way up to the kitchen. Mrs Noah had prepared a special supper to celebrate Noah's birthday. The meal was rounded off by a large fruitcake. Mrs Noah said that she had put six hundred and one raisins in it, but nobody was able to count them.

"Six hundred and one raisins to be thankful!" said Noah with a twinkle in his eye.

Everybody groaned. Noah was always making bad jokes.

Before making up his log that night, Noah counted the marks that he had cut with his knife on the wall of the cabin. Yes, this really was his birthday.

He turned over the page, and began to write:

Year two, first month and first day.
Weather – fine and bright.
What better day to remove the covering of the Ark? The whole family joined in the work of cutting away the hides that covered the roof. All the animals are enjoying the lighter, fresher conditions.
Special supper to celebrate my six-hundred-and-first birthday. Such a delicious fruitcake.
My boys tell me that I am getting

old, but I don't really feel any older
than when I was five hundred and one!

## CHAPTER 17

# A New Beginning

It was almost two whole months after the roof came off that Noah began to feel that God was happy for them to come out of the Ark at last. They all knew that this operation was going to have to be done carefully.

The plan was to tie a strong rope to a large basket and lower one of the boys over the side of the Ark and down to the ground. His job would be to work out where to cut a new door in the side of the boat, so that the people and the animals would be able to leave the Ark in an orderly way.

Although Noah's boys were now grown men, each of them wanted to be the one to go down in the basket and be first to walk on the ground.

"All right," said Noah, "we will draw straws to see who goes first."

He chose three stalks of hay, all of different lengths. He gripped them in his fist with only the tops showing.

"Right boys. Shortest straw goes first." It was Japheth who took the shortest straw.

They rigged up a pulley, so that they could gently lower the basket over the side of the Ark. Japheth climbed into the basket and held tightly to the rope. He had with him a long, two-handed drill. His orders were to drill some holes right through the wall of the Ark, so that the others could find the place from the inside.

For Japheth, this was more fun than rolling down a grassy hillside. The basket swung to and fro as it went down. He could see the marks of the waterline on the big black hull of the boat, and the barnacles and bits of seaweed that had grown there. Looking down, he could see the ground coming ever closer.

No sooner had the basket bumped onto the ground, than Japheth was off. Leaving the drill in the basket, he ran and jumped and cheered, punching the air with his fist. The rest of the crew watched as he disappeared into the distance.

"I hope he's coming back," said Shem. But soon they caught sight of a little figure jogging along toward them.

"It's great to be back on solid ground!" Japheth shouted up breathlessly, when he reached the Ark.

"Come on, son," Noah shouted down to him. "Stop messing about. We've got work to do."

So Japheth went round the Ark a few times, looking for a suitable place to cut a new door. He settled on a place where the ground was rising gently. He could see that it would be a simple matter to build a slope with the rocks and stones that were close to hand. He drilled the first hole, and the others went down below to see where it had come through.

Eventually, after a lot of shouting to one another, and a few more holes, they worked out where the door should be. Then they set to work with saws, chisels, and axes to make an opening big enough for all the people and animals to use. As soon as it was big enough for a cat to get through, Clysmic started making a fuss, so they passed her through to Japheth. She immediately jumped from his arms and set about exploring this beautiful fresh new world until the hole in the wall of the Ark was big enough for the people to fit through. The family came out one by one and walked around in wonderment. Everything smelled so green and fresh. It was a miracle.

Noah couldn't stop himself from crying. It wasn't that he was sad; it was just that he was so relieved that here they all were, safe and sound, back on dry land.

Noah recorded that day in his logbook. It was the second month of his six-hundred-and-first year, and the twenty-seventh day. The whole voyage had taken them one whole year and ten days.

## CHAPTER 18

# Freedom for the Animals

The next major task for Noah's family was to let the animals go free. It would be no good just to open the doors and let all the creatures find their own way out into the fresh green world. That would be chaos, and some of the small creatures would get squashed.

They started with the birds. As the roof was now missing, it was a simple matter to open the cages and let the small birds fly away. It was such fun watching them go. Some of them had long journeys ahead of them, so they would need to wait until they were strong and fit enough to go. Many of them knew that they would not be staying here very long. Soon they would be flying far away beyond the distant mountains.

Then it was the turn of the large birds. Some of them had to be helped on their way. Then there were the birds that would be useful on Noah's new family farm – the ducks, the geese, the chickens, and of course, Noah's doves. All these would have to wait until they had new houses to live in.

Last of all, it was the turn of the fierce birds. Some of them flew off at great speed, enjoying their freedom. Others spread their great wings and soared up into the sky until they disappeared from view among the clouds.

The four-legged creatures were next. Once again, the crew started with the small ones. Many of these had increased enormously in number during their time on the Ark. The family put them into baskets and carried them far away from the Ark. They let them go where they could find good hiding places and plenty to eat.

Then came the large animals. God was giving them a new, strange feeling for the humans who had cared for them over the past year, and for this great big black ship that had kept them from disaster.

As soon as they were out in the open, they could smell the fresh plants and trees all around them. They could see the whole country stretching out before them to the distant horizon. It was then that a feeling of panic rose up within them. All they wanted to do was to get away, and keep running and running until they felt safe again.

The farm animals were different. The sheep, goats, and cows were happy to stay with Noah and his family. They would be the beginning of all the creatures that would be such a blessing to the people of the world for all the years that stretched out ahead of them. They somehow seemed to know that they and their offspring, and the many generations that followed, would be happy to live and serve alongside the humans who would farm the lands that they could see spread out all around. They knew that they would be content with that life.

Last of all came the fierce animals. Noah knew that these creatures would be an important part of the new world that was beginning. They would help to keep the wild animals fit and strong. They would catch and eat the weaker ones, so that only the strong and healthy ones lived to have young.

Noah had been careful to carry only young ones of these creatures with him in the Ark. They were all now a whole year older and bigger, so the men led them well away from the Ark before they let them go. But they need not have worried, because God had put the same feelings about the humans in them too. Suddenly they were afraid of people. As soon as they were released, they simply raced away.

## CHAPTER 19

# A Promise and a Sign

As soon as the job of releasing the animals was complete, Noah and his family felt that they should have a special feast to celebrate this new beginning and to thank God for saving them and all the animals. They wanted to share the feast with him, so they built an altar out of the stones that were lying about the place. Then they carried the big table and chairs all the way down from Mrs Noah's kitchen and set them out upon the ground near the altar.

They spent most of the day preparing the feast, so it was getting late in the afternoon when things were ready.

First, they gathered round the altar and roasted some of the best joints of lamb for God. Everybody watched as the smoke of the fire and roasting meat drifted up into the sky. As they stood, looking up and smelling the delicious smoke, they said prayers of thanks to God.

Then Noah began to sing the family song, which they knew so well:

> *"The Lord is good.*
> *His faithfulness reaches to the heavens.*
> *The Lord is good.*
> *His love endures for ever."*

They sang it again and again, and then, joining hands, they began to dance round the altar, singing as they danced.

It was a cloudy day, and as they danced and sang, a little rain began to fall. The sun came out just above the distant mountains. The golden light shone through the falling rain.

Suddenly, there appeared in the sky a beautiful rainbow. It stretched right over the Ark, a great arching stripe of vibrant hues that reached from one side of the sky to the other. No one had ever seen anything like it before. They stood and watched for a long time, until the rain stopped and the rainbow faded away.

Then they turned and looked at one another, their faces wet with the rain, and their eyes full of joyful tears.

"God is speaking to us," said Noah. "He is saying that he will never flood the Earth like this again."

Noah looked round at his family. He pointed up to the sky, where the rainbow had been shining just a few minutes before. "And this beautiful arc will be a sign for him and us. It will remind him of his promise, and all of us of his great love and faithfulness."

"It looks like an upturned boat," said Mrs Noah, looking at her husband with her eyes full of tears.

"So it does, my dear," replied Noah. "God is saying that since there will never again be such a dreadful flood, we won't be needing the Ark anymore."

## CHAPTER 20

# Comfort

After a long, thoughtful silence, Mrs Noah spoke up.

"Let's serve up the food," she said.

"Yes, my dear," said Noah. "Let's celebrate this special occasion."

So they took their seats at the table. Mrs Noah went from one to another ladling helpings of the wonderful tasty stew, which she had been keeping warm on the fire. There was fresh bread to dip into it, and plenty of nuts and raisins from the store-rooms in the Ark. There was mint tea to drink, and wine and sweetmeats enough to keep them going until the sun went down, and the moon and stars appeared in the sky above them.

So they all drifted back to the Ark and up to their cabins. They felt warmed and comforted by the wonderful meal. Their hearts were full of wonder and thankfulness to God.

Before he settled down for the night, Noah took out his logbook, and started a new page:

> Year two, third month, fourteenth day. Weather – sunshine and showers. A day of celebration and thanks to our faithful God.
>
> Today, a great and wondrous sign appeared in the clouds – an enormous curved stripe of radiant light stretching across the sky over the Ark. It was made of many beautiful and vibrant hues. We have never seen such a marvel in the sky before.
>
> Our God has made a new promise to mark this new beginning.
>
> "I promise that I will never again put the Earth under such a terrible curse. As long as the Earth exists, there will be a suitable time for planting, and a suitable time for harvesting. There will always be a pattern of cold and heat, summer and winter, day and night."

So Noah and his family began to live and farm in this new world into which they had arrived. They brought out all the seeds that they had carried with them in the Ark. Some they had forgotten to label, so it was a matter of sowing them to see what would come up. They ploughed, harrowed, planted, and finally, harvested.

All the cows, sheep, and goats had calves, lambs, and kids. The ducks, geese, and chickens hatched lots of ducklings, goslings, and chicks. Even Shem, Ham, and Japheth and their wives all had children. Everything was multiplying.

When Noah gathered in the crops of wheat, barley, and maize at harvest time, and when the family started gathering the fruit from the trees, filling their baskets with olives, grapes, oranges, and apples, Noah said to his wife, "I wish my old dad could have seen this. It would bring him such comfort."

# Epilogue

## How is Noah's Story known today?

Many people think that it was Moses who wrote the story of Noah, but it is a bit of a puzzle to know how he knew so much about this amazing tale.

When Moses was a baby, he was hidden in a waterproof basket and floated among the reeds that grew at the edge of the River Nile in Egypt. (This basket might be called "Moses' Ark"!)

Nobody knows what Moses was called at first, but he was discovered by a princess. She was the daughter of the king of Egypt. She liked the look of this little baby, and decided that she would keep him herself. She called him Moses.

Thanks to his cunning sister Miriam, Moses was looked after by his own mother, who was paid by the princess for caring for him. He grew up among his own people, and then when he was old enough, Moses went to live in the royal palace.

As he grew, he was educated by the best teachers in Egypt. He learned to read and write in Hebrew, and he learned the Egyptian language and culture.

Books were rare and expensive in Moses' time, but Egypt was a very wealthy place, so the palace might well have had a good library.

When he was a grown-up man, God asked Moses to lead his people to freedom. They had been slaves in Egypt for many years. The other important thing that Moses did was to write five books, which were included in the Bible. The first of these is called "Genesis". This is where the story of Noah can be found.

Nobody knows how Moses knew so much about Noah. People have come up with all sorts of ideas, but because there is so much detail in the Bible about Noah and the exact dates when things happened on the voyage of the Ark, it looks as though Moses had a book to work from.

It has always been the custom for a ship's captain to keep a daily record of everything that happens on board. This is called the "ship's log". It is very likely that Noah did the same, but what happened to that logbook? It is something of a mystery.

Maybe one day a merchant came to Egypt from far away, with lots of interesting treasures that he thought the king might be interested in. Perhaps the king came across a quaint little book among the items for sale, which his scholars told him looked like a ship's log, and so it was added to the palace library.

Who knows?

# Postscript

The story of Noah is more important than you might think. Here is a list of other places in the Bible where it is mentioned: 1 Chronicles 1:4; Isaiah 54:9; Ezekiel 14:14, 20; Matthew 24:37–38; Luke 3:36 and 17:26–27; Hebrews 11:7; 1 Peter 3:20; and 2 Peter 2:5 and 3:6.

What Noah did makes a wonderful story, but just as Jesus told us stories to help us understand more difficult things, so we can use this story to help us understand other things in the Bible.

You might like to think of ways in which Noah was like Jesus. Think about these bits of the story:

- *The world is suffering from a dreadful curse, so God gives Lamech and his wife a baby boy.*

- *Noah is given a difficult job to do, but he does everything that God asks of him.*

- *Noah works with wood.*

- *The Ark is made of wood and nails. It saves people from God's judgement.*

- *When Noah's voyage in the Ark is over, God makes a new start for his family, with a brand-new promise (or covenant).*

- *God gives a sign or token as a reminder for Noah and his people.*

- *The new life for Noah's family begins after a soaking in water. (See 1 Peter 3:19–21.)*

- *The next time we see a rainbow in the Bible, it is around the throne of God in heaven. Ezekiel sees it in a vision, and so does John, many hundreds of years later. (See Ezekiel 1:28 and Revelation 4:3.)*

You might be able to think of more ways in which Noah's story helps us to understand God's mysterious ways.

# ALSO AVAILABLE

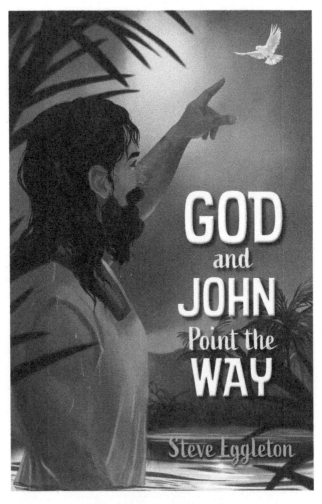

ISBN: 978 0 7459 7949 6